The Amazing A to Z Scripture Adventure

The Amazing A to Z Scripture Adventure

Sharon Jordan

Table of Contents

Copyright Information

The Amazing A to Z Scripture Adventure
by: Sharon Jordan

Published by:

Good News Fellowship Ministries
220 Sleepy Creek Rd.
Macon, Georgia

ISBN-13: 978-1-7344999-2-6

Format by : Lisa Walters Buck

Dedication

This book is dedicated to the unique and incredible students and joyful, God-filled teachers who came through the doors of Agape Faith Christian Academy from 2001 to 2006 and to my wonderful friend, Hope Tillotson who opened the door for me to have those five years of treasured memories, spiritual growth, and friendships. I love you all!

To the Students

If you are reading this, my prayer has been answered. I asked God to reach out across the miles and find every one of you and put this little book in your hands. And here you are! I have missed you!

Over the years that have passed, we have all had life experiences that have shaped us into different people from who we were at AFCA. For some of you, the short time that you were there is a distant memory if you remember it at all.

I am hoping you'll be able to find your way back in your memories and enjoy moments of fun, laughter, joy, and simpler times: the long lunches, kickball played way too rough, video lessons fast-forwarded way too much, circles and chapels that carried us into the Presence of God.

I'm praying that you will see your life as it is now through the innocence of your childhood and through the eyes of God Who sees the end from the beginning. No matter how far from Him you have gone or how far away He seems, He is as close as the whisper of His name. I am praying that our beloved A to Z verses will come back to embrace you and give you more joy, strength, and peace than you have ever had before.

I love you each very much and treasure the time I had with you. I would love to hear from you. God is with you.

-Mrs. Sharon

In Loving Memory

For the joy you both brought our
way,
You reached heaven before the rest
of us!
We love you!

Mrs. Maryjane Mote
(Elementary Teacher 2002-2006)
Katheryn (Gourley) O'Shaughnessy
(1st grade 2001-2002)

Introduction

"Fill up with My Word, and My Life will flow into every area of your life."

When I heard these words from the Lord many years ago, I saw a picture of something you might see in a science lab. It was an upright clear tube with branches coming out of each side. I drew a picture of this on an index card and labeled each branch: family, church, work, ministry, friends, business. I had favorite verses that I memorized and meditated on throughout the day. As I visualized His Word pouring into me from the top, I could see His amazing Word flowing into each area of my life.

When I began to teach school at our church school, I knew the Lord was leading me to teach His Word to the students. We learned a verse for every letter of the alphabet, and reviewed these so often that every child from kindergarten through 8th grade could easily quote the verse and reference when prompted with any letter of the alphabet. I like to think that every one of those students could do well at this even today.

My prayer is that each of you will have an experience with these 26 versus plus 5 Power Verses that will change your life forever. Each day you'll grow closer to God and full of His Word. His words will flow into every area of your life every day of your life and you will be enriched for the rest of your life!

"Fill up with My Word, and My life will flow into every area of your life."

The 100-A-Day Adventure

In the following pages I will introduce you to 31 dear friends of mine that will in turn reveal to you the very life of Jesus and give you the gifts that He has for you. Spending time with them is spending time with Him.

If you are willing to make this gift of your time and energy, each verse you learn will come alive for you and bring life to you.

Here's how it works:

As I introduce each day's verse, spend the day with it meditating it, repeating it over and over. Set a goal of repeating it to yourself or out loud 100 times. You may not make it at first, but the more you meditate it, the more you will want to.

I will repeat this message many times in the Tips of the Day: Exercising your spirit is much like exercising your spiritual body. Repetition is key. The value of disciplining yourself to get your 100 reps in each day will be invigorating more than I can say. You have to experience that thrill for yourself. It will be a spiritual adrenaline rush when you reach your 100 reps in a given day. Then do the same for the new verse each day. If you have ever enjoyed the benefits of physical discipline, wait until you experience the benefits of this spiritual discipline. After the first month of rigorous, exciting adrenaline-pumping success, you'll probably want to take on the Extreme Adventure.

The Extreme Adventure

After you have completed "The 100-a-Day Adventure," please take "The Extreme Adventure." Take a verse each week and spend the entire week with that verse, still trying to say it 100 times each day. By the end of that six month period, you'll be ready to do it again, and you'll be reviewing and meeting with your friends everyday. You'll be meditating the word of God day and night. You'll have success greater than you could have imagined in every area of your life.

Nestle in with the verse of the week. Explore it, meditate it, love it, learn it, and enjoy it. With the Extreme Adventure, you can get through all A to Z verses twice in a year. You will be refreshed, strengthened, and unstoppable!

Thanks for joining me on this amazing adventure. Let's go!

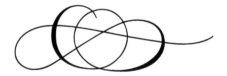

A is for "Asking"

Ask and you shall receive that your joy may be full. John 16:24

Allow me to introduce the very first verse of our Amazing A to Z Scripture Adventure. Tah-dah...

The "A" verse has been with me since July of 2001. I had met this verse in church a few times and knew we would become lifelong friends. "A" became real to me the summer before I started teaching at our Christian school in North Carolina.

It was the first one of 26 verses that I knew I would teach my students. My idea was that they would have 26 verses that they could call their own. If awakened in the night, they would know these verses so well they could quote them from their heart without even being fully awake. These verses would become a part of them and would be with them all of their lives.

Our friend "A," also known as John 16:24, virtually covers every need anyone could have. It promises that God will answer your every request and every question. You just have to ask. This is not a slot machine verse where you just say, "I want this, and I want that." This is a relationship verse. If you look at this amazing verse in the context of John 16, you will see that because of Jesus' relationship with His disciples, He made a way for them and for us to get all of our questions answered and have everything we need if we ask.

Remember, this is not a slot machine verse. It is a relationship verse. God was confident that the Spirit of Truth living in us would guide us into all truth. This means we would be wise enough to ask the best questions and to receive the best answers. We would learn to listen to our heart for the answers rather than seeking answers only through our reasoning.

We can ask questions all day long, learn to hear His answers, and receive His guidance. We have the Wisest One available to us at all times and willing to provide the answers we need.

As we get this verse in our heart, we will know how to ask and what to ask. We will receive, and our joy will be full!

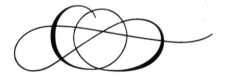

Tip for the day: As a trigger to help you remember, say this verse or think it every time you open a door today. Say it or think it ten times each time. As you open the door, picture yourself opening to the answer to your question or problem.

It takes an incredible number of repetitions and meditation to get a verse in you, but it will be the greatest return on your investment of time you have ever had.

And Now a Joke Just for Fun:

A fellow was praying one day and feeling very close to the Lord, so close he felt he could ask Him any question and he would get an answer. So he looked up to heaven and asked the Lord, "Lord, what is a thousand years like to you?" The man was startled when he immediately heard the Lord say, "My son, a thousand years is like a second to me." The man was encouraged and asked another question, "Lord, what is a million dollars to you?" The Voice of the Lord boomed from heaven, "A million dollars, my child, is like a penny to me." After a brief pause, the gentleman humbly looks to heaven and asks, "Lord, will you give me a million dollars?" The Lord's voice rang out, "Just a second."

We will soon learn to ask the best questions! Enjoy your day with "Ask and you shall receive that your joy may be full." John 16:24

Getting to know "B" tomorrow might just be the best thing that has happened to you in a long time!

B is for "Benefits"

Blessed be the Lord who daily loads us with benefits, even the God of our salvation. Psalm 68:19

On this second day of The Amazing A to Z Scripture Adventure, I present to you Psalm 68:19. I affectionately call it the "B" verse.

Here's a truth, we should all know and remember:

What we focus on, we attract!

"B" is telling us to focus on our blessings! If we count our blessings, we will have more. If we focus on everything that is wrong, the measure of our misery increases. When our eyes are open to the goodness of God, He will show you what you have been missing! Walk with "B" and you will stay tuned into the blessings all around you. You will attract more blessings to you.

God is delighted when He finds someone who will focus on and acknowledge the benefits He gives. Giving is His nature, and He truly wants to bless us more. The one He can bless more is the one He can use more to bless others. It's a cycle of love and giving that brings glory to His name!

"B" is dear to me because it is one we printed out on a big sheet of paper and taped to the dash of the car. The boys and I would say it ten times each time we got in the car. Once, 5-year old Nick received a twenty dollar bill from a well-known traveling minister, and he was certain it was a result of having meditated this verse.

Blessed be the Lord who daily loads us with benefits, even the God of our salvation. Psalm 68:19

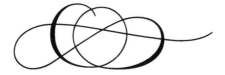

Tip of the Day: Remember you are trying to meditate each verse 100 times a day to get well acquainted with it. Today as you say it, picture your blessings with a grateful heart. You can look around the room and be glad for everything you see. When was the last time you thanked God for the chair you're sitting in? Celebrate everything today, and you'll sleep well as you rest from the party of gratefulness you've had all day!

Have a terrific day, loaded with benefits, and get ready for tomorrow because "C" will set you free.

C is for "Carefree"

Cast all your care upon Him, for He cares for you. I Peter 5:7

What are you worrying about today? Is it one thing, two things, or three. Sometimes it seems like hundreds when it's really only one or two. You may feel that if those cares would go away, you would be happy and at peace again, yet they are very real to us. They scream for attention and solutions. Cares can sometimes make you feel paralyzed. You don't feel like doing anything or talking to anyone. You are weighted down as if you were carrying a sack of rocks and trying to run a race. The more you rehearse the cares you have, the heavier they feel, and the worse you feel.

"C" tells us that there is Someone who doesn't want you to feel this way. There is Someone who wants you to win your race. He volunteers to take your cares. He'll carry your sack for you and will reveal creative ways for you to turn them inside out. He can turn a rock into a blessing as easily as He turned water into wine, walked on water, and cast out demons. Let Him have your cares and see what He can do with them. He will run alongside you as you cross the finish line and win your race every day of your life.

"C" will become your best friend as you feel lighter, more energetic, and productive. You have a beautiful and exciting day ahead of you that you can enjoy with family or friends or people you meet. Don't wait another moment. Hand over the whole sack at once or one care at a time. And as daylight turns to evening, you will feel the waves of God's goodness wash over you and give you peace.

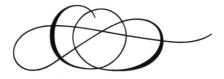

Tip of the Day: "C" will be there for you all day if you will focus your attention in that direction consistently. Can you think and say your "C" verse 100 times throughout the day today? Yes, you can. Cast your care every time you say it, and by the end of the day, you'll be walking on air! Give it a try. I know you'll be glad you did!

Tomorrow "D" is going to offer you something delicious!

𝒟 is for "𝒟elight"

Delight thyself also in the LORD; and he shall give thee the desires of thine heart. Psalm 37:4 (NIV)

As we continue our Amazing A to Z Scripture Adventure, here's dynamic and diverse "D."

It is very difficult to keep from smiling when you think about "D." There are so many things you can delight in and so many ways to demonstrate delight. "D" will show you how to delight in the Lord.

"Mmmmmmmm!" Your eyes are closed, the spoon is held in midair; it has just left your mouth. What was it? It was something "delightful." That is obvious from your expression. Perhaps key lime pie with all its tartness, or was it a warm brownie with melting ice cream or flaky apple pie. You really are enjoying that aren't you? That's what it means to "delight." It is savoring an experience, devouring it to receive every morsel of its goodness. It is allowing yourself to forget everything else but this one thing for the moment.

"D" invites you to savor Someone much more glorious than a piece of pie. At first, I loved Psalm 37:4 for the wrong reason. It was all about me getting what I want. "D" taught me to savor Him and His goodness and then "what I want" becomes what He wants for me. Then He fulfills the desires of my heart. To my delight, I find out that that's what He wanted for me all along!

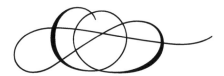

Tip of the Day: As you smile through your day with "D", let some of your repetitions simply be the first four words: Delight in the Lord. Imagine what that looks like. Imagine His Presence; think about His love, His power, His goodness. Savor Him. Delight in Him. Your desires will get lost in your delight, and you will find that all you really want is Him!

Tomorrow "E" has somewhere to take you. Don't miss out!

E is for "Enter"

Enter into his gates with thanksgiving, and into his courts with praise: be thankful unto him, and bless his name. Psalm 100:4

You've made it to the fifth verse of your Amazing A to Z Scripture Adventure. I hope you are beginning to feel that these verses are your friends.

Before you take a closer look at "E," please take a peek at the whole family. They are known as the five verses of Psalm 100. You are going to love these guys. "E" will take you by the hand and lead you right into God's presence. The rest of the family members chime in to encourage you to joyfully praise the Lord.

Psalm 100 KJV:

(1) Make a joyful noise unto the Lord, all ye lands. (2) Serve the Lord with gladness: come before his presence with singing. (3) Know ye that the Lord he is God: it is he that hath made us, and not we ourselves; we are his people, and the sheep of his pasture.

And here's our "E":

***(4) Enter into his gates with thanksgiving, and into his courts with praise: be thankful unto him, and bless his name.** (5) For the Lord is good; his mercy is everlasting; and his truth endureth to all generations.*

If God has a gate (and He does), I want to go through it. If God has a court, (and He does) I want to be there. "E" tells us how to do it, so let's go.

We enter into His gates with thanksgiving. Each thankfulness we offer up to God is a stepping stone into His presence. Each praise we offer takes us into His court.

Hold "E" close to your heart as you offer up praises today and enjoy the wonderful, magnificent Presence of the Lord as He sets you free.

> *I thank you, Father for your blessings in my life. Thank you for health, life, friends, and family. Thank you for my job, my home, your Word, your truth! I praise you for Who You are! You are my Lord and Saviour! You are mighty to be praised. I give you glory and honor. I lift up your name in all the earth. I praise you! I worship you! You are awesome, O Lord!*

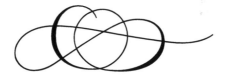

Tip of the Day: Using your imagination, can you see yourself going right on into His Presence, praising and thanking Him. How long can you keep praising Him? Will you run out of things to thank Him for? You might even try thanking him for things that start with each letter of the alphabet to help you keep going. Here's what that could sound like:

*Lord, I come into Your presence praising and thanking You. I thank You for **apples**, their juiciness and flavor. I'm in **awe** of the **beauty** you have **created** on the earth and in my heart, I thank you that you take all of my **cares**. I can **cast** my cares on you. I thank you for every **day** that you give me and for what you **do** for me in one day. I thank you for **elephants**, **eagles**, and the ability to eat and good **food** to eat. I thank you, **God**. that You reign in my heart.*

That was easier and more fun than I thought. We could do this everyday and never run out of things to praise Him for! However you choose to do it, be sure to enter into His presence with thanksgiving and praise. There is no better place to be!

Now that you have five whole verses in your heart, practice by doing what each verse tells you to do. For "A," practice asking. For "B," count your blessings and benefits. Whenever you think of "C," cast your cares on Him. "D" exhorts us to delight in Him, and "E" inspires us to be thankful to Him and bless His name.

Thanking God and entering into His presence: What a great way to spend a day, and a lifetime!

When you come by tomorrow, many of you are going to meet an old friend. "F" is going to remind you of how much you are loved!

F is for "Found"

For God so loved the world, that he gave his only begotten Son, that whosoever believes in him should not perish, but have everlasting life. John 3:16

Ahhhhhhh, finally a verse you already know; the beloved John 3:16 is our "F" verse. It was very likely the first verse you ever learned if you attended Sunday school as a child. Even if you gave your heart to the Lord later in life, "F" may have been the very first verse that was shared with you.

John 3:16 is tightly knit. It completely and compactly gives us God's plan of salvation for every person in the world. It's all there. . .who, why, what, when, and how. It's all we need to know to make our way to God and literally have eternal life beginning right now.

God's love is far greater than our love for our children, grandchildren, mothers, fathers, sisters, and brothers. He thought of us, created us, created a world for us, and then gave us authority over everything in it. We are His project, His plan, and His purpose. All of His dreams, hopes, and plans are wrapped up in us. His greatest desire is for us to find Him and believe in Him so He can give us eternal life.

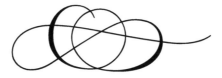

Tip of the Day: "F" is one of the most beloved and well-known verses in the Bible. Be sure you know it well! Try saying each part of this verse 10 times and then stop to picture it in your imagination.

1. *For God so loved the world... I see his eyes of love looking at me.*

2. *He gave his only begotten son... Jesus is on the cross paying the ultimate price so that we can know His Father.*

3. *That whosoever believes on him... I see myself kneeling before Him believing, loving, trusting Him. I picture other people I know looking up at Him believing, trusting, and loving Him.*

4. *Shall not perish but have eternal life... I see myself coming out of the darkness and into His light, knowing the wonderful life that is ahead of me forever with Him.*

Eternal life starts now!

Bonus from "F"

"F" tells us that whoever believes in Him shall not perish. The Greek word for perish is "apollumi" which actually means "to lose or be lost." To get a picture of John 3:16 revealed by this interpretation of the Word, come with me into the forest by way of your imagination:

You are lost in the forest, wandering aimlessly, lost and alone. There are many twists and turns, rocks and stumps to trip you. That tree suddenly looks very familiar. You realize you are going in circles. You thought you were making progress, but you are back right where you started. "Help!" you yell. It's soon going to be dark, and there are going to be scary animals, bears, coyotes, maybe even snakes crawling around on their way to dinner. You don't want to be the one to satisfy their appetites. Your imagination starts to run wild. Your breathing becomes heavy; you are frightened and sweating. You are overwhelmed and not at all sure you will make it out of here alive.

Then you hear a quiet voice saying your name. You turn and look to your left. It's not quite dark yet, and you can barely make out a face. He is coming to you, and He is calling your name again. You are calming down and feeling better. Hope is returning. When He is close enough, He asks you to believe in Him. You allow Him to lead you out of the darkness and away from all of the scary things. As He walks with you, He makes sense of all of the twists and turns, and as daylight comes, He shows you His beautiful creation. Together you explore the wonders of the woods that moments ago frightened you so much. You are in awe of all that you missed when you were afraid and alone.

He leads you out of the woods into a beautiful meadow. You sit by a stream under a huge live oak tree. You discuss your dreams and plans and His dreams and plans for you. You marvel at His wisdom and kindness. He shows you how to take the next step and the next. He shares even more of Himself with you until you can barely breathe with the wonder of it! This is eternal life.

You are going to have a fabulous day with the Lord today! It is wonderful to know that eternal life starts now!

Are you wondering what "G" offers you tomorrow?

G is for "God Has Given"

*God has not given us a spirit of fear,
but of power and of love and of a
sound mind. 2 Timothy 1:7*

Getting to know powerful "G" is going to put more power, love, and peace in your life.

It will really pay you to flex your spiritual muscles and get this dynamic verse in your heart. It will set you free from fear and make you strong enough to win every battle. "G" entrusts us with three of the most extravagant gifts God has, but first He takes away the main force that prevents us from walking in power, love, and a sound mind.

No Fear

God doesn't ever give you fear. He wants you to be powerful against the enemy. He gives you a spirit of love. Fear can't stay. Perfect love casts out fear. With "G" in your heart, you can say "goodbye" to fear and embrace God's power, love, and sound mind.

Power

"G" tells us that God has given us power. Think about that for a while. God has given us power over the enemy, power to be free and set others free, power to change the atmosphere, power to change circumstances, and power to change the world! Marriages can be restored, children can be saved, depression can leave, and healing can come, all because of the power of God in us.

Love

"G" tells us that God has given us a spirit of love. Love conquers all. When our words and actions come from love, everything changes. Love enables us to stay calm and think the best of others even if they do wrong to us. God's love changes us. God's love is the driving force that will change the world.

Sound Mind

God gives us a sound mind. With a sound mind, we are in peace; we think clearly; we know what to do. A sound mind sees things from God's perspective. Chaos and confusion are in the past. Right thinking and God's thoughts lead us in paths of life.

God gives us power, love, and a sound mind. Receive it all by meditating this verse today.

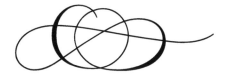

Tip of the Day: As you get to know "G" today, focus on what God has given you. "God has given me a spirit of power, love and a sound mind." I suggest that you say that part of the verse 4 times to every 1 of "God has not given me a spirit of fear." This will emphasize what you have, and put fear in its rightful place: right out of your life.

Yes, It takes hard work to become physically strong. We must build our muscles by doing hundreds of reps on expensive equipment and faithfully pay for a membership to a fitness center and actually USE it on a regular basis. Being strong and powerful in the spirit is no different, though less expensive. In fact, it's free of charge. All we have to do are hundreds of repetitions of life-filled and energy-charged words from God. When we pay that price, our spiritual muscles are strengthened, and we become unstoppable. With His power, we can take down any and every enemy. Pay the price today to get this verse firmly implanted in your spirit. God needs you powerful, loving, and at peace!

ℋ is for "ℋealing"

He sent his word and healed them and delivered them from their destruction. Psalm 107:20

Say "Hello" to "H." It is huge in its life-giving potential. "H" will bring you healing! Let that soak in for a moment! You can receive your healing as you meditate "H" today.

When we said this verse as a class, we changed "them" to "us" and one of our joyous students would always lead us to put the emphasis on "us." (I can hear you now, Heather.) It's important to know that Jesus came to heal US and deliver US from destruction.

Make no mistake about it: God wants you healed in your body, mind, and heart. Yes, there may be many things you will learn through the time of infirmity; learn them well. Draw close to God and to His word in your infirmity. Know that He wants you healed and delivered.

While they are praying for their healing, many people get impatient and frustrated. Many even give up. Many more are not sure that it is God's will to heal them. "H" and many more verses from the Bible tell us the truth.

"H" brings with it patience and grace for this time of infirmity. Healing may come instantly, or it may take some time. We want to spend that time continually thanking Him for His healing and deliverance so that there is no doubt in our mind. Doubt can keep our healing at a distance. Every word of faith and thanksgiving takes us closer to our healing.

God is waiting for us to catch up to what He has already provided. We do that by meditating "H" until we believe it. "V" and "W" will tell us more about this later, but for now "H" is whispering healing to you. Receive it. God wants you healed and wants you close enough to Him that He can touch you and breathe life into you no matter what circumstances are currently upon you. They are temporary; He and His deliverance are eternal!

Your healing will be a life-giving testimony to others and will empower you with an anointing to pray with authority. Your healing is not just for your benefit; it will have a ripple effect on many others.

Immerse yourself in "H" today and receive your healing and all of the benefits that come with it.

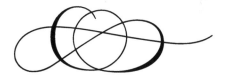

Tip of the Day: Meditate Psalm 107:20 today. Believe and receive its truth, and you will be healed and delivered from all destruction.

We don't experience Truth because it is in the Bible; we experience Truth because it is in us!

> *My prayer, as I write this, is that this book goes around the world to find those who need God's healing in body, mind or heart. He is not limited in time or space, and He will find you because He wants you healed.*

"I" is an incredible verse that you'll get to meet tomorrow!

If you are disrespectful to God and others, are you in position to be blessed?

If you are aggravated and frustrated, even if you feel you have reason to be, are you in position to be blessed?

The good news is:

If you're being grateful for where you are now, you are in position to be blessed.

If you are praising God and worshipping Him continually, in spite of your circumstances, you are in position to be blessed.

I is for "If..."

If you are willing and obedient, you shall eat the good of the land. Isaiah 1:19

Incredible "I" has a simple message for us:

> ## Get in position to be blessed.

"I" asks theses question:

If you are continually looking at your problem and talking about it, are you in position to be blessed?

If you are arguing and complaining, are you in position to be blessed?

If you start everything you say and do with love, you are in position to be blessed.

If you let Hope rise up by thinking about solutions, answers and fulfilled dreams, you are in position to be blessed.

If you are patiently anticipating the good that God has planned for you, you are in position to be blessed.

If you are willing and obedient, you are in position to be blessed.

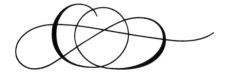

Tip for the day: This is a short one so it's easy to say it, sing it, or think it a hundred times today. It's going to be more helpful if you know what "the good of the land" is for you. Think about what your promised land looks like, and then declare this: I am willing and obedient, and I eat the good of the land!

Then all you have to do is be willing to receive it and obedient to whatever God tells you to do next!

Be thankful for this thrilling promise today and hold a picture of your very own "good of the land" in your imagination. Have an extraordinary day!

Tomorrow "J" is going to tell you something amazing that Jesus did!

𝒥 is for the "Name of Jesus"

Jesus called his twelve disciples together, and gave them power and authority over all devils, and to cure diseases! Luke 9:1 (ISV)

What an amazing thing Jesus did that day in Luke 9:1. He gave his disciples power and authority over demons and diseases! Because He tells us in His Word that we will do greater things than He did, we know that He also gave you authority! You can do it! You have power and authority.

You are not powerless! With the name of Jesus, you have power over demons and diseases. Don't let them walk all over you or your friends or have any influence in the things that affect you. JESUS says you can drive out demons and heal diseases. Let's pay attention to what He said!

When we said this verse at our school, we would often end it by enthusiastically shouting, "Power and Authority, Power and Authority, Power and Authority!" It has to sink into our thick human heads that God has given us power and authority! Can you picture yourself with your "super power" suit on? Mine is blue and white and has "Jesus" across the front of it and a giant "J" on the cape! That is locked safely in my imagination, of course.

If you doubt that God has given you power and authority, study these scriptures:

Matthew 18:18-20 ESV

> *"Truly, I say to you, whatever you bind on earth shall be bound in heaven, and whatever you loose on earth shall be loosed in heaven. Again I say to you, if two of you agree on earth about anything they ask, it will be done for them by my Father in heaven. For where two or three are gathered in my name, there am I among them."*

Find some Power Buddies and start binding and loosing according to God's perfect will!

As we ponder "J" today, let's meditate the name of Jesus. It is He who has given us power and authority. Don't get sidetracked by thinking you are going to get glory for this, but don't think for a moment that He doesn't want you walking in authority! As "J" gets in your heart, you will pray and live your life with power and authority, and you will do great things in His name!

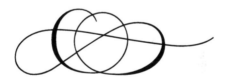

Tip for the day: I challenge you to take the limits off. Know that God wants you doing greater things than Jesus did. He trusted you with power and authority, and He expects you to use it. Don't hold back! Do something powerful in His name as you meditate "J" today.

Can you hardly wait to unveil the treasure that "K" has for you tomorrow?

$\mathcal{K}$ is for "$\mathcal{K}$eep"

"Keep your heart with all diligence; for that is where your life comes from." Proverbs 4:23 (paraphrase)

A friend of mine calls his wife, "Special K," and she is, but Proverbs 4:23 is my "Special K." "K" is so special because it answers the frequently asked question, "Why?" Why is one person successful and another one is not? Why is one person miserable and another one not? Sometimes two siblings raised in the same home with the same parents take two separate pathways. "K" tells us that what is in our heart determines what our life will be like.

We have to understand "K" to know how to have abundant life. God has given us the responsibility and privilege to determine this ourselves. With His help and guidance, we will make the right choice.

We know from Proverbs 23:7 "As a man thinketh in his heart, so is he." What you see, what you hear, what you say, and what you think, all go into your heart. What you keep in your heart is your choice. Those daily choices determine the life you live. You must watch your heart diligently and allow only those things that you desire that are true and good to be kept there. Those things you focus on, repeat, and give affection to will produce fruit in your life, good or bad.

Nestle up close to "Special K" and let this secret be revealed in your life as you make right choices and live the life God wants you to live.

Your very life depends on it.

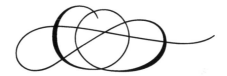

Tip for the day: Be excited about putting this energizing verse in your heart today. Saying this verse 100 times will remind you that your life comes from what you keep in your heart. Guard it with all diligence!

"L" has a real surprise for you tomorrow! You won't want to be late!

ℒ is for "ℒight"

*Let your light so shine before men,
that they will see your good works,
and glorify your father which is in
heaven. Matthew 5:16*

"L" is coming to us bringing a surprise. If I told this
to you myself, you wouldn't believe it, but coming from
this Source, I'm sure you'll accept the truth of it, once
you hear it a few times.

God wants your good works to be seen by men!

I don't know about you, but that surprised me. I was
taught to do everything undercover, and there is certainly a time and place for that, but we must eagerly
embrace "L" and know that God wants your good works
to be seen by men so that your Father will be glorified.

We don't do acts of kindness to be seen by men, but God wants men to see our kindness. He wants us to act like Christians. Act like Jesus. Let His love come through in the things you say and do.

Getting to know "L" will actually cause us to glow with the power of this word. We have a choice to make. Let it shine or not. We can turn the light switch on or off. At any time, we can choose to act exactly like everyone else we know. We can act in such a way that no one would suspect us of being a Christian. We can fit right in with the world: talk the talk and walk the walk. No one will feel challenged to live better. They will have no one to turn to for help and no one to show them the way. Or. . .we can be different. We can smile when there is no reason to smile. We can be calm when everyone else is upset, and we can reach out and lend a helping hand when it's not convenient. It is totally up to you and I every minute of the day.

We can look for needs to fill. We can pray for opportunities to love. The more we think about Jesus as we go about our day, the more His love will show through our actions. The more we act like Jesus, the brighter our light will shine. Others will notice, and God will be glorified because we have shown His love to those who need it so desperately.

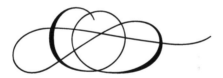

Tip for the day: If repeating "L" or any other verse seems boring or seems to produce nothing, keep repeating it. Even if you are not really thinking about it, keep repeating it. Even if you feel you're not hearing what you're saying, keep repeating it. It is going into your heart. This life-giving Word will come back to speak to you and will produce God's power, truth, and life within you. This Light will shine brightly, and others will see it and glorify God.

Enjoy your day, letting your light shine.

M is for "Merry"

"A merry heart does good like a medicine." Proverbs 17:22

"M" is one of my best friends because I love to laugh and in general just be happy. Feeling "merry" is much to be preferred over having a "broken spirit."

"M" exclaims, "A merry heart does good like a medicine!" It goes on to tell us what happens when we are not merry. A broken spirit dries the bones. That doesn't even sound healthy.

Since health and happiness are so scripturally tied together, why are we taught to ignore our feelings. Our feelings shout at us all of the time. They affect how we think and act. "M" suggests that we should pay attention to our feelings. Having a merry heart is as important as taking medicine.

What pharmacy will fill my prescription for a merry heart? How can I get one if I am miserable? I have good news for you.

The kingdom of God is within you. Luke 17:21

And the kingdom of God is righteousness, peace, and joy in the Holy Spirit. Romans 14:17

Not only do your thoughts follow your feelings, but your feelings follow your thoughts. God has placed this tremendous power within you! If your thoughts gravitate to the kingdom of God within you and all of the good God has placed in your life, I promise you, as God has promised you, your feelings will follow along peacefully! You will be amazed at how taking control of your thoughts can help you find your merry heart.

Casting down imaginations, and every high thing that exalteth itself against the knowledge of God, and bringing into captivity every thought to the obedience of Christ. 2 Corinthians 10:5

Finally, brethren, whatsoever things are true, whatsoever things are honest, whatsoever things are just, whatsoever things are pure, whatsoever things are lovely, whatsoever things are of good report; if there be any virtue, and if there be any praise, think on these things. Phillipians 4:8

Here's an important truth:

We are happy, not because everything is great and everything is going our way, but because He is great, and He is showing us the way.

When you get to know Jesus, your heart will smile! You realize that it is God's plan for you to be happy, that he wants you to be happy, and it's important to be happy! Happiness will make everything better. It tastes good going down. It will bring healing to your bones. It will bring joy to your relationships. A merry heart does good like a medicine. Say that as much as you can. That's what the Great Physician Himself prescribes.

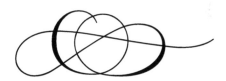

> **Tip of the Day:** Go ahead and laugh out loud while meditating "M." There are a lot of extremely funny ways to look at life and circumstances. Not taking life and people so seriously paves the way to a merry heart. Good things happen when we smile, and even more when we laugh.

I suggest that you and "M" find some fun in everything you do today. Be lighthearted, happy, and excited about what comes your way.

I know it is not always easy to maintain a merry heart, but by meditating this extraordinary truth God will reveal ways to find joy in your circumstances and truly live with a merry heart.

I hope "M" will become one of your best friends. Its medicine will work wonders for you!

Tomorrow you'll find out what "nothing" does!

N is for "Nothing"

Nothing can separate us from God's love. Romans 8:38 (NLT)

Nothing, zero, not anything can separate us from the love of God.

Right before our "N" verse in Romans, you will find a long list of what can't and won't separate us from God's love. Here's Romans 8:35 from three versions of the Bible:

Who shall separate us from the love of Christ? shall tribulation, or distress, or persecution, or famine, or nakedness, or peril, or sword? Romans 8:35 KJV

Who shall ever separate us from Christ's love? Shall suffering and affliction and tribulation? Or calamity and distress? Or persecution or hunger or destitution or peril or sword? Romans 8:35 AMP

Do you think anyone is going to be able to drive a wedge between us and Christ's love for us? There is no way! Not trouble, not hard times, not hatred, not hunger, not homelessness, not bullying threats, not backstabbing, not even the worst sins listed in Scripture: Romans 8:35 The Message

When the students and I said this verse, it had a jingle to it. I wish you could hear it. We said it like this, "Nothing ca-aan separate us from God's love," and then each student would call out something that "can't separate us from God's love." They would randomly pick something and shout it out. Then we would do the verse again. They could choose anything that came to mind, and sometimes it was a unique thought. Here's what it sounded like:

"Nothing can separate us from God's love."

"Not the devil!"

"Nothing can separate us from God's love."

"Not Drugs!"

"Nothing can separate us from God's love."

"Not Death!"

"Nothing can separate us from God's love."

"Not Sickness!"

"Nothing can separate us from God's love."

"Not Cotton Candy!" (?) I know, but that's the kind of thing that could come out of a child's mouth.

Meditating on *God's love and knowing that nothing can separate us from that love will change us!*

When the enemy of your soul tries to convince you that God does not love you, remember what Romans 8: 31-39 says, and "N" declares loudly.

> *When I am afflicted, He still loves me!*

> *When someone stabs me in the back, He still loves me!*

> *When I am bullied, He still loves me!*

> *When calamity befalls me, He still loves me.*

He still loves me when I face: Destitution, distress, famine, hard times, hatred, homelessness, hunger, nakedness, peril, persecution, suffering, and even the sword.

When tribulation comes upon me, He still loves me.

When trouble comes, He still loves me.

Even the worst sins cannot separate me from the love of God.

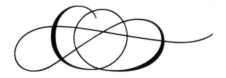

Tip for the day: When you're saying "N" today, put a little rhythm to it. It will take on a character of its own and seep into your heart more quickly. Then try to make a list of things in your daily life that won't separate you from the love of God!

Look forward to the next letter because everyone wants to meet "O".

O is for "Oh, Thanks"

O give thanks unto the Lord; for he is good: for his mercy endureth forever. Psalm 136:1

I am thrilled to introduce you to "O." "O" comes out strong as the very first verse of Psalm 136. In fact, it is so strong, it is repeated three times in the first three verses of Psalm 136.

*1) O give thanks unto the LORD; for **he** is good: for his mercy **endureth** forever. 2) O give thanks unto the God of gods: for his mercy **endureth** forever. 3) O give thanks to the Lord of lords: for his mercy **endureth** forever.*

As you can see, David thought of this idea of repetition long before I did. Repetition is the key to getting an idea, a truth or really anything into your heart. We definitely want to get "O" into our hearts.

Today with "O" can be a day of thanking God all day! Is that possible? Observant Jews would give us a resounding, "YES!" According to Mark Batterson in *Double Blessing*, they are known to say a blessing before, during, and after a meal. They believe "a man should taste nothing before he utters a blessing." Orthodox Jews won't just say, "Thanks, God." They will make a proclamation:

"We give thanks unto You for every rain drop You caused to fall on us."

"Blessed be he that created this bread."

"Blessed be He who makes strange creatures."

Observant Jews will say at least 100 blessings a day, taking notice of everything they experience throughout the day and thanking God for it. We can do the same!

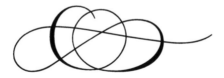

Tip of the Day: Will you take that challenge? As you meditate "O", make a proclamation of blessing for anything and everything you experience today, for He is good and His mercy endures forever. You can also use the tip from "E" and be thankful from A to Z all day long. That has become one of my favorite ways to praise, thanking him for something that starts with each letter of the alphabet as I praise through the day.

You'll see how the "bad" transforms to good every single time because you are focused on how good He is! His mercy endureth forever.

"P," the twin brother will be along to visit tomorrow with a very similar message!

𝒫 is for "𝒫raise"

Praise ye the Lord. O give thanks unto the Lord; for he is good: for his mercy endureth forever. Psalm 106:1

If you liked the "O" verse, you are really going to love "P"! "O" and "P" are identical twin brothers with just one phrase to tell them apart.

106:1 *Praise ye the Lord. O give thanks unto the Lord; for he is good: for his mercy endureth forever.*

136:1 *O give thanks unto the Lord; for he is good: for his mercy endureth forever.*

Getting the most out of these twins is so simple. All you have to do is say them and do them. While "O" is a great reminder for thanking God for all He has done for us and blessed us with, "P" reminds of what He has redeemed us from. For Israel and for me, that is plenty.

Psalm 106:1 rests at the beginning of a list of Israel's sins, iniquities, and wickedness, ranging from complaining to worshiping the image of a calf. His mercy endureth forever.

I haven't worshipped the image of a calf, but I am grateful that He took my punishment for the sins I have committed when He made the ultimate sacrifice. Here's my list:

- *Worrying*
- *Fear*
- *Demanding my own way*
- *Anger*
- *Complaining*
- *Focusing on my own desires over the desires or needs of others*
- *Being quick to judge others*
- *Gossiping*
- *Pride, and sometimes even worse.*

Praise the Lord. Oh give thanks unto the Lord, for He is good. His mercy endureth forever. I have placed every one of these sins under His blood. Through His grace and mercy, I have been redeemed. Most of the time these days, I act like it. Praise be to the Lord forevermore. "P" reminds us that no matter how far we have fallen, He has always been and will always be there to pick us up. Praise the Lord forevermore.

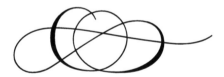

Tip of the Day: As you go through today with "P," continue to thank Him for every blessing you encounter. Also, if you dare, notice those times that you fall short, make mistakes, or sin. You have a choice to make each time:

You can berate yourself and give attention to your shortcomings or choose a second option: ask forgiveness, and then praise the Lord. Give thanks unto Him for His mercy endureth forever.

"P" and I suggest you wisely choose the second option and give glory to God. These weaknesses can then become our strong points as we give testimony to what He has done in us. Let the twins be a part of every day and see what God will do!

"Q" is going to answer a very important question for you tomorrow.

Q is for "Quench Not"

Quench not the spirit. I Thessalonians 5:19

This phenomenal little four-word verse may be the most important one of all! Put another way, it says this:

Allow the Spirit of God to flow.

We can quench, or we can allow. It's our choice. We do this every day. The Spirit of God is like a river flowing; don't try to dam it up or stop the flow. Flowing means without effort or struggle.

What stops the Spirit of God from flowing without effort through us?

Negativity, doubt, fear, worry, selfishness, anger, strife, over-thinking, a critical spirit, lack of focus or expectation.

What allows the Spirit of God to flow freely through us?

Focus, expectation, praise, thankfulness, obedience, prayer, meditating His Word, listening for His Voice, pursuing peace, finding joy.

If you remember "G," you know that God has given us a spirit of power, love, and a sound mind. Imagine this: "Q" allows the spirit of power, love, and a sound mind to flow through you. Whatever you do, don't quench the spirit of power, love, and a sound mind. Get excited about what you can do by allowing the spirit of God to flow through you today!

Quench not the spirit; let the river of life flow through you.

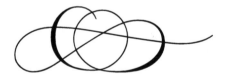

Tip for the day: Make this declaration as you stretch yourself to say this verse 100 times

"I allow the spirit of God to flow freely through me today."

Spending time with "Q" will help keep you in the flow of His life-giving Spirit.

Tomorrow our likable friend, "R" will make you smile.

R is for "Rejoice"

Rejoice in the Lord always: and again I say, rejoice. Philippians 4:4

My friend, "R" is certainly in the running as my favorite simply because it means: **"Dare to be happy!"** It means step out and rejoice even if circumstances are contrary to what you want, even if it is not easy to find something to rejoice about. "R" tells us to "Rejoice in the Lord always!"

Why did God tell us to rejoice and to rejoice again?

Here's "R's" answer: For one thing He wants you to be happy. He wants you to rejoice. Secondly, He knows it's good for you to rejoice. It's good for you to look on the bright side of things. God is the ultimate optimist! He already knows everything's going to turn out just right! He thinks it's pretty important that we go ahead and get excited about what the future holds. He thinks it's important to look at all the blessings that we have instead of fretting over what we have not.

He says rejoice and rejoice always and rejoice again. He knows we can if we try. Even when things look their bleakest, we can rejoice. It is possible to rejoice even when we don't feel like it. He'll take our hand and show us the way. Let's rejoice in the Lord and let's rejoice with the Lord, then we can be happy today and every day!

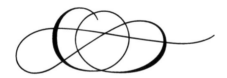

Tip for the day: Today's tip is to put a smile on your face, change what you've been thinking about, and rejoice in the Lord. It will be the best gift you can give yourself and others.

As an added bonus, here's a testimony from someone who was rescued by "R" one dreary day.

*"On the way to work this morning, I said Philippians 4:4 about 50 times, and I said it 50 times again on the way home. **It rescued me.** I hadn't had the best day in the world. Negativity had tried to overshadow me. Different scenarios played out in my thought life from numerous angles threatening to plunge me into discouragement and hopelessness. I even lost sleep. I hadn't experienced this type of attack in quite awhile.*

After saying the verse, "Rejoice in the Lord always, and again I say rejoice," 50 times, I can't say I noticed a significant change in my attitude; I didn't suddenly hear angels singing. All I can say is, at some point I noticed I didn't feel as negative as I had. I began to feel stable instead of about to fall over the cliff. As it turned out, I had a successful day business-wise and still felt stable at the end of the day. I can't say I felt totally excited and joyful, but I felt strong, peaceful, and steady. I felt at rest."

This is a testimony to the life that is in one verse of scripture. All he did was repeat the verse without even trying to get something out of it or do anything special with it. **He just said it.** The life of God is in His Word.

I challenge you to take a chance with "R." Say it, think it, write it, sing it. Imagine what your life will feel like when "R" changes you. If you stay close to "R," you'll be opening the door to the answers you seek!

Dare to be happy! Rejoice in the Lord always, and again I say rejoice.

Coming up next: If you like singing, you're going to love "S".

S is for "Sing"

Sing unto the Lord a new song. Sing unto the Lord, all the earth. Psalm 96:1

Say "Hello" to "S." This good friend of mine is sure to get you singing if no other verse has. You can't just say this verse, you have to sing it. You have to smile. You have to lift your heart in joy to the Lord. There's another verse I love to think about when singing,

"All the trees of the forest sing for joy." Psalm 96:12 (NIV)

Picture that, and then lead the trees and the earth in singing to Him. You can see why this is such a delightful verse to know. Singing will give you that merry heart we talked about!

Keep singing until your heart takes over and sings for you. Whether you know what you are singing or not, keep singing unto the Lord. Let Him have all your burdens and cares. Open your heart to hear Him singing back to you.

Your heart will be lighter, and your joy will be full. Sing unto the Lord all the earth.

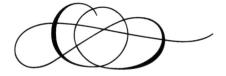

Tip of the Day: I know it sounds crazy, but I encourage you to try singing today. Just sing what comes to mind and then keep singing about God and His magnificent splendor! This morning, I sang out about how the Lord made heaven and earth and all that was in it. I sang about how He made something out of nothing, and then I sang about how He could take my nothing and make it something. It was a new song, and it changed me.

Remember to say your verse over and over up to 100 times each day; this is what gets it in your heart so you will have this friend to forever remind you to "sing unto the Lord!"

Have a glorious day!

Get excited! Tomorrow you get to meet "Mr. T."

'Tis for "Trust"

Trust in the Lord with all your heart and lean not unto your own understanding. In all your ways, acknowledge him, and he shall direct your paths. Proverbs 3:5, 6

Once a man was taking a leisurely walk in the mountains enjoying the beauty of God's creation when suddenly he stepped too close to the cliff and found himself falling toward certain death. On his way down, he frantically reached out for a tree limb hanging just within reach. He held on as best he could, knowing that without divine intervention, he would plummet to his death.

"Help!" he cried out. "Help me, please!" He continued to yell for help and finally called out, "Is anybody up there?"

Then he heard a voice saying, "Yes, I'm here."

"Who are you?" the desperate man asked.

"It's the Lord!" he heard a booming voice reply.

"Can you help me," he asked while his hands began to slip from the branch.

"Yes, I can help."

"What do you want me to do? Help! I'm falling!"

"Let go of the branch."

Looking around the man became full of panic. "What? You've got to be kidding!"

He heard the instruction a second time. " I am the Lord. Let go of the branch. I will catch you."

"Uh... Is there anybody else up there?"

Trusting: it's easy to talk about, not so easy to do.

Our friend, Mr. "T" is going to have you relaxing more, overthinking less, and struggling very little.

The "T" verse has three magnificent parts to it.

Three magnificent parts:

1. Trust in the Lord with all your heart. *Let go of the branch. Saying things like, "It's all going to work out." "God will take care of it," and "He will show me the way," are great ways to show trust.*

2. Lean not unto your own understanding. *Our "reasoner" is faulty at best. I can trust Him for the answers instead of trusting my intellect.*

3. In all your ways acknowledge Him, and He will direct your paths. *Keeping my eyes on Him is the best way to end up where I want to go.*

Trusting:

The key to this entire verse is in trusting "with all your heart." Often we think we are trusting when we are still holding on to doing it our way. We are trusting with part of our heart. When we trust with all of our heart, we get our mind and heart in unity, completely and whole-heartedly renewed to trust in Him. Then miraculous things happen.

We have the confident assurance that everything is going to work out for our good. We are bullet-proof. Nothing can disturb our peace. No one can hurt us. Everything is going to work out just right! We know that our loving heavenly Father will see to it. He wants what is good for us, and He has the power to see that the very best comes out of every circumstance for us. We trust God.

Leaning:

Lean not unto your own understanding. Years ago, I was very fortunate to hear the Lord speak to my heart very clearly. I know it was Him because I don't talk or think like this, and it surprised me. It started me on a path to freedom from overthinking. Deep in my heart, I heard His voice say, "Your reasoner is faulty at best." I have laughed at myself many times over the years as this statement has proven true numerous times! I am much better off leaning on His answers than I am when I'm leaning on what comes from my faulty intellect.

Acknowledging:

In all your ways acknowledge Him, and He will direct your paths. It's great to get a conversation going with God. Ask Him what He thinks about everything from the weather to what's for lunch to what's happening in the world. Acknowledge that He is with you more certainly than any other being you can see. He hears your thoughts and feels what you feel. Simply let Him know you know He is there. Keeping my eyes on Him is the best way to end up where I want to be.

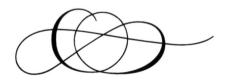

Tip for the day: As you get well acquainted with "T," declare this:

I trust you God. I trust you!

Your mind must be renewed to this truth so that you trust him with your whole heart. Then meditate each of the three parts of "T" separately before putting it all together. When we walk in all three parts of Proverbs 3:5,6, we are demonstrating what life in the Spirit of God looks like. Mr. "T's" message is simply "Trust, lean, and acknowledge." You can be sure God will take care of the rest!

U is for "Unto You"

Unto you, O Lord, do we give thanks.
Psalm 75:1

If you are ever discouraged, down and out, and looking for peace, "U" is the one to guide you. There's nothing quite like being thankful if you want sunshine back into your life. As you change focus from all that is wrong, a glimmer of hope will shine through. As you keep on counting all you have to be thankful for, the sun will shine brighter and brighter for you.

I read of a man who took the challenge to thank God for daily miracles. Because he had a biology degree, he thanked God for aerobic respiration, mitochondria, creating ATP, glycolysis. Then he began to thank God for all of the amino acids by name. He would have named every bone in his body if he had known them. Honestly I can't remember when I've thanked God for my femur or tibia. This gentleman spent the day praying continually as he tried to name every single thing he could think of that he was currently experiencing. He ended up totally in awe of God's miraculous intervention with His creations.

"U" encourages us to do the same thing in our own way. We can become aware of everything going on around us and in us and through us that we often take for granted. Here's part of my list:

My relationship with God
My family
My home
My job
My friends
My family and the way I was raised
The privilege of homeschooling my boys
Being blessed with the world's best husband
My children
The relationship they each have with the Lord
My three precious daughters-in-law
My granddaughters and grandson and more to come

Many adventures, and overcoming opportunities throughout my life. . . I'm giving thanks unto the Lord for all of these things right now.

I am thankful most of all for the huge blessings of salvation, the Blood of Jesus, and the certainty of heaven. We could spend every day and probably should spend every day being thankful for those things. I have undying gratefulness that I can have a personal relationship with God through His Son Jesus and have the Holy Spirit to comfort, help and guide me.

As we declare our gratefulness to God, there will be a smile on our faces and peace in our hearts. The atmosphere around us will be charged with joy, and those we come in contact with will be blessed.

I'm up for the challenge of rekindling a thankful attitude. For unto you, O Lord, do we give thanks. . .for the big and the little, the tangible, the intangible. You are God of the universe; you made everything within it. We bless your holy Name!

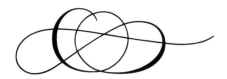

Tip for the day: If you have continued your Scripture Adventure from A to U, you now have become acquainted with 21 new friends. Were you able to commit all of them to memory yet? If not, "U" is a good one to start with since it only has 8 words. I encourage you to stretch these next few days and memorize the verses.

My life is so rich because these verses are a part of me. It's exciting to hear them mentioned from the church pulpit and know they are mine! My heart shouts, "That's my verse!" I want you to have this experience, and it starts with knowing them "by heart." Today make sure you know "U" really well as you give thanks. You will never regret the time you are spending memorizing and loving the Word of God.

V is for "Verily"

Verily, I say unto you, whosoever shall say unto this mountain, Be thou removed and be thou cast into the sea: and shall not doubt in his heart, but shall believe that those things which he says shall come to pass, he shall have whatsoever he says. Mark 11:23

"Are you kidding me?"

"You can't be serious!"

"That's incredible!"

"Are you sure that's in the Bible?"

"Why have I never seen that before?"

These are all common exclamations you might hear from people who are meeting "V" for the first time. Here you find 47 words packed with a truth that can totally turbocharge your life!

Out of those 47 words, can you find the 12 dynamic words that epitomize what Jesus is saying to us in Mark 11:23?

> *Verily I say unto you, whosoever shall say unto this mountain, be thou removed, and be thou cast into the sea; and shall not doubt in his heart, but shall believe that those things which he says shall come to pass; he shall have whatsoever he says.*

12 Vital Words

Whosoever shall say, and shall not doubt, but shall believe, shall have.

And in 3 words:

Say, believe, have.

I didn't say it. My pastor didn't make it up. Abraham, Isaac, and Jacob didn't invent this idea. Jesus said it! I know you don't like the idea of "name it and claim it." I don't either. In my opinion that is some man's phrase for making the Word of God sound like something we should run away from. Instead of running away from this verse, I want to run to it.

I have embraced Mark 11:23, and I have said it more than any of the other verses except for its neighbor, the "W" verse, which we shall soon talk about. We know that the person who "names it and claims it," leaving God out of the equation, will end up spiritually poor. "V" declares the person who says it and believes it. . .receives it. "V" is a very good friend to have. You will marvel at the miracles God has made available to you.

With "V" as your friend, you make a difference in your world for the glory of God by saying, believing, and having. Praise the Lord forevermore!

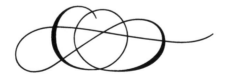

Tip of the Day: If you haven't done this yet, consider making verse cards to take with you or put them on your mirror, refrigerator or in your car. For review have someone call out a letter, and give them the verse for that letter. We used to begin and end our school day in a circle, and students would call out a letter. The class would then respond with the verse. That is still a great way to begin and end any day.

Remember "V" was God's idea! Don't be afraid of it! Run with it!

"W" walks right along beside "V" with a powerful truth!

$\mathcal{W}$ is for "Whatsoever"

Whatsoever things you desire, when you pray, believe you receive them, and you shall have them. Mark 11:24

I proudly and excitedly announce "W." "W" is a huge friend, well-known for its far-reaching effect on mankind. "W" is unstoppable; "W" reaches to the outer edges of possibility to bring the seemingly impossible into the realm of the possible.

"W's" message is so incredibly expansive. Whatsoever includes everything you can think of. It includes everything and anything you desire. "W" gives three simple steps to get you started toward your "whatsoever.

1. *Decide what you really want.*

2. *Pray.*

3. *Believe.*

And you shall have them.

We thought, as good Christians, it doesn't matter what we want; it only matters what God wants. "W" says it matters very much to God what we want. He cares very much and is extremely interested in what we want. He wants us to have what we want. Wow for "W!"

How can this be true when we are so often selfish and greedy? The key is in the praying. Praying purifies our desires. God is the Ultimate Optimist. He is confident that when we pray, our "wants" will line up with what He wants. Don't underestimate the love of God for you personally. We have to catch up to where He is in His faith in us. When we are one with Him as He desires, we can be trusted with the desires of our heart. Don't be afraid to believe He wants good things for you.

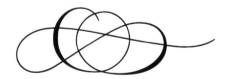

Tip for the day: As we are moving toward the end of the alphabet, don't forget the importance of repetition. Everyone who is physically building their body knows the importance of consistency and constant repetition, stretching yourself beyond what you think you can do. Reaching for that 100 reps for each day's verse is just like that, but the dividends will be eternal. You keep on going whether you see a difference on any given day or not. Keep on keeping on day by day because the word of God is doing the work in you. It is sharper than any two-edged sword. You will experience a strong and healthy spirit that God can use to move mountains.

Bonus from "W"

"W" is full of promises, here's a bonus message that highlights the believing part that "W" wants you to understand. You can read this later if you're simmering with the "Whatsoever."

Now read "W" again: "Whatsoever things you desire, when you pray, believe that you receive them, and you shall have them." Mark 11:24

It doesn't say believe that you are going to receive them. It doesn't say hope you receive them, or that you should wish you would receive them. It says to believe you receive them (with the implication being receive them right now.)

How do you "believe you receive them," and what does that really mean? It means you believe you have it when you pray. It means doubt is gone, and you enjoy the emotions you would have as you actually experience what you prayed for. It's that real to you. This is a truth that is contrary to what the mind can accept on its own. The reality of this truth will be revealed as we meditate upon this Word. Jesus is telling us to believe that we have the answer to our prayer now, not in the future.

How can we go from doubt to belief? I have meditated this question along with this verse for years, and I am still searching and praying for that answer. It starts with imagining what we could accomplish if we did not doubt.

The following is a list of ways we can build our faith, get rid of doubt, and believe we receive now. Try some of them, and you will find yourself going from doubt to belief.

1. *Pray and listen to what God is saying to you about what you want.*

2. *Say the right things. Talk about what you want.*

3. *Picture it in your God-given imagination.*

4. *4Believe and say, "It is possible for this to happen."*

5. *See the end result. How will you feel when it happens the way you want?*

6. *Thank God for it in advance.*

7. *Let your imagination run away with you. Create the image of what you want and go with it.*

8. *Be positive in all things. Practicing seeing the best of every-thing, every person, and every situation puts you in position to believe that good can come to you.*

9. *Meditate the scriptures that tell you God wants to bless you and answer your prayers.*

10. *Ask God to help you believe.*

11. *Think about what you believe. Start small, and your belief will build.*

12. *Realize what an important part thinking has to do with believing. Try substituting the word "think" where this verse and other verses use the word "believe." The revelation you get may surprise you. It may surprise you even more when you begin to "think right," and find that you now "believe right." That is when you will find that you can now speak and act "right."*

13. *Take a step in the right direction. What is one small thing you can do to move in the direction of what you want?*

Believing you receive now is a very important facet of your Christian life. Most Christians are living far below what God had intended for them. Have we been deceived by the enemy of our soul to keep us from doing all God wants us to do and having all He wants us to have? God wants us to have the desires of our heart, whether that be health, healing, prosperity, safety, soundness of mind, peace, positive relationships, salvation for our loved ones, or any other thing that is in our heart.

As we meditate "W", let's allow our heavenly Father to take us from doubt to belief in at least one specific area of our lives. Choosing to get doubt out of the way leads to a life of true adventure.

Enjoy a day of believing and receiving!

Expect greatness when you meet "X" tomorrow!

X is for "Exalt"

Exalt the Lord our God, and worship at his holy mountain; for the Lord, our God is holy. Psalm 99:9 (NIV)

Drum Roll, please. . .Introducing my friend, "X." "X" invites you to come to the holy mountain and worship the Lord. There's nothing more beneficial than spending the day at the holy mountain exalting God.

We exalt His name and worship at His holy mountain because God is Holy. The more time we spend in His Presence, the more like Him we will be! As I considered this verse, I became increasingly uncomfortable with the idea of being holy. When I mentioned to my husband that I was writing about holiness and how farfetched the idea of being holy is to me, he calmly, confidently commented, "That's what Jesus is for!" And I know he's right. Jesus was sent to cover our sins so that we could be made holy.

We exalt Him because He is perfectly perfect and blameless. He cannot sin. He does not lie. He is full of love, mercy, and grace. When we worship Him at His mountain, we will have the mountaintop experience of seeing Him as He is and seeing ourselves as He sees us. Let's go to that mountain every day!

Embracing "X" will help us be holy like God wants us to be! How glorious that is! We exalt the name of Jesus forever for making this possible for us!

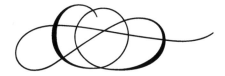

Tip for the day: Remember you want to allow this verse to become a part of your daily life, and repetition is the key. Think it, or say it, as you wake up. Think it throughout the day and as you fall asleep at night. Say it out loud when you can. From the connection that is made through familiarity, the truth of the verse will be revealed to you by the Holy Spirit. He will speak to you through it. You will be amazed at the life that is in one verse of the Word of God planted in your heart!

Check in to meet "Y" tomorrow. My friend "Y" will let you know just how important you are to the world.

Y is for "You"

You are the light of the world; a city on a hill that cannot be hidden.
Matthew 5:14

Here's my friend "Y" and here's what he has to say to you:

You are the light of the world: a city on a hill that cannot be hidden. People are watching you. They are stumbling around in the dark, confused, insecure, and frightened. They may look and talk like everything is great with them, but many don't even know there is a better way. They really need the light. You have to shine.

Here's what the world is saying to you:

"Somebody, turn the light on, please. I can't see where I'm going, and I don't know what to do or who to turn to.

What's that glimmer of light I see as I get close to you? Now I can see better. I won't trip over things. I won't be deceived so easily. I will understand spiritual things better. I can maneuver around the obstacles in my way so I won't stumble and fall. I can see exactly where to walk, and I'll not be bumping into things like I did before. Your light is helping me see things more clearly.

I see how it's supposed to be now that your light is shining. I can see now how I'm supposed to act when things go wrong in my life. You show me how I'm supposed to treat people that I don't agree with. I see how I'm supposed to treat my family members. I see. Thanks for keeping your light on so I can see the way."

Sometimes you'll hear the world say, "Please show me how to have a light shining out of me the way you do!" And that, my friend, is what we live for!

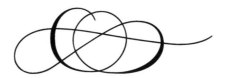

Tip for the day: The more we meditate "Y" and know we are the light the world needs, the brighter our light will shine. It's not something we have to try to do; He just shines through us as we focus on Him. Declare: I am the light of the world, and the world needs my light.

Tomorrow "Z" will wrap up our zealous adventures in the spirit!

Z is for "Zechariah"

"It's not by might, nor by power, but by my spirit says the Lord."
Zechariah 4:6

"Z" is here to wrap things up for us. When I was on my search for a "Z" verse, you can imagine my fruitless efforts to find a verse beginning with "Z." When I found this one, I knew it had to be included! You will never regret knowing and living with "Z" as your friend.

"By My Spirit." Three little words packed with power and backed with the authority of God Himself!

You've got to love "Z" because it makes everything so much easier and so much better! It's not by might. It's not how hard you try. It's not by power, how strong you are, or how great you are. It's by His Spirit. It's by God's Spirit, His power, His might, and His authority, not our own.

What could be better news? We don't have to do it. We don't have to be strong. We don't have to be mighty. We don't have to have it all together. We don't have to be powerful or smart because He is. Let go of it. Let God do it. "By His Spirit" is the secret to living an amazing life every day for His glory!

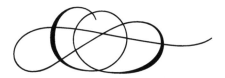

Tip for the day: As we meditate this today, we're going to let go, and we're going to let God do what He wants to do through us! And it's going to be amazing! After all, it was by His Spirit that He created the world and all that's in it! It's by His Spirit that He sent Jesus to die on the cross and raised Him again from the dead. It's by His Spirit that He draws all men to Himself and equips us to be His Love upon the earth. By His Spirit!

The Power Verses

A to Z are now friends of yours, but since we have 31 days in many of our months, I brought along 5 more powerful friends to strengthen you as you finish out the month. Once you get to know them, you won't have to leave home without them.

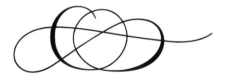

Power Verse One: Strength

I can do all things through Christ who strengthens me. Philippians 4:13

I don't have to say much about any of these "guys" because they speak for themselves. Get to know them by heart, and try to say them 100 times in a day. You will be empowered in ways you can only imagine!

You can say this verse all day long and feel the power surging through your spirit. Power Verse 1 leaves no room for discussion about where that power comes from and neither should we. We always give God the glory for the great things He strengthens us to do. He is our source always and forever, and without Him we could do nothing. With Him, we can do everything! No limits! Go for it!

Tip for the day: Use this trigger: Every time you see someone in a red shirt, think or say this verse ten times. Can you find ten red shirts today? Let the red make you think "I'm Dynamite!" because this verse will give you all the power of God you need for today. Know that "You Can!"

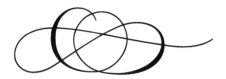

Power Verse Two: Abide

If you abide in me, and my words abide in you, you shall ask what you will, and it shall be done unto you. John 15:7

John 15:7 will stand by you when you really need a friend. After you have Power Verse 2 in your heart, you'll get answers to your prayers. I know this because it happened to me! There was something I really wanted to happen, and one day I realized I had not ever asked God to do anything about it. It was a problem that needed to be solved. I had to take action that I was afraid to take because of fear of rejection. Instead of stepping out and doing something on my own, I remember very well meditating this verse over a hundred times that day. Then I prayed, then I took action, then I got my answer. 1, 2, 3. . . It worked just that way.

This is a powerful verse, and it will see you through anything and everything you face. God's answers always meet your deepest needs, even those you don't know you have. Abide in Him; it is the best and safest place you can ever be!

Tip for the day: John 15:7 assures us that we have been doing the right thing all along as we have taken our thought time to meditate 28 verses so far! We are doing exactly what Power Verse 2 tells us: abiding in Him and opening up so that His word abides in us. Be confident in your prayers today. God will answer your prayers! Remember:

God has an answer to every prayer.

He has a solution to every problem.

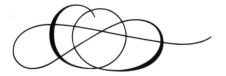

Power Verse Three: Peace

Thou wilt keep him in perfect peace whose mind is stayed on thee because he trusts in thee. Isaiah 26:3

I was in college at Southern Wesleyan University in the little town of Central, South Carolina when I first met this verse. It was love at first sight. I was away from home for the first time, and I was way out of my comfort zone.

As I first walked into the dormitory, my eyes were drawn to a large picture frame over the piano in the lobby. The brown mahogany frame encased this comforting verse. To my knowledge, I had never heard that verse before. I was astonished to realize that it was in the Bible. It was profound. It held the answer to life's big question:

Where can I find peace, and how can I hold on to it once I find it?

I recently talked with someone who told me they had searched for peace their whole life. This person is about 28 years old and had been raised in a difficult home. I had known him for only a brief period during his life, but he made an impact on me. As I recently reconnected with him, I was intrigued with what he told me. I have since prayed consistently that he and others I know would find this wonderful peace.

This one verse offers the way to peace for us all! It means getting our eyes and our mind off of the problems and circumstances in our lives. It is getting our eyes and our mind off of people who disappoint us, let us down, or even abuse us physically or emotionally. It is getting our mind off of people who appear to be hypocritical, deceitful, hateful, or mean. It is getting our mind on God, His word, His Son, and His love for us!

Power Verse 3, my favorite verse, tells us that we will have peace if we keep our mind on Jesus because we trust Him. We may not ever trust another person on the earth, but if we trust Him and keep our mind on Him, we will not only be okay, we will have peace.

This to me is the greatest truth of all time:

Jesus offers us real and everlasting peace.

Tip for the day: Today wear blue for peace. Every time you think about blue today, think or say Power Verse 3, Isaiah 26:3. I promise it will be a good friend to you. It will direct you to peace and the only One Who can give it to you.

Two more days. Two more power verses. Are you considering the 6-month Extreme Adventure with your A to Z's?

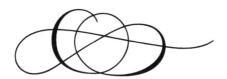

Power Verse Four: What God Hates

There are six things the Lord hates—
no, seven things he detests: haughty
eyes, a lying tongue, hands that kill
the innocent, a heart that plots evil,
feet that race to do wrong, a false
witness who pours out lies, a per-
son who sows discord in a family.
Proverbs 6:16-19 (NLT)

Power Verse 4 comes with some power-packed information. These days many people seem to believe God
is okay with just about anything a person wants to do.
Proverbs 6:16-19 tells us the truth.

God wants to fill every part of our lives, but He can only fill up what is not already occupied. He will fill us with His love, His power, and His grace, but if we have areas in our life that harbor the sins He hates, He cannot fill it.

By giving ourselves wholly to Him on a daily basis, He will come in and fill us, and all of the sin that He hates will be replaced with His love, power, and grace.

Let's memorize these 48 words, and as we do, let's ask God to clean our hearts of anything that He detests. Keep renewing your mind to the truth that He, and He alone, forgives our iniquities and makes us a new creature in Christ. Feel the refreshing that comes from drinking of this cleansing water.

Tip for the day: Today, let's go with the red shirts to represent the blood of Jesus. When you see someone wearing red today, that's our reminder to meditate the 4th Power Verse and claim the cleansing blood of Jesus to make room for all God has for you.

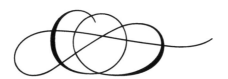

Power Verse Five: Think

"*Finally, brethren, whatsoever things are true, whatsoever things are honest, whatsoever things are just, whatsoever things are pure, whatsoever things are lovely, whatsoever things are of good report; if there be any virtue, and if there be any praise, think on these things.*"

Power Verse 5 tells us how to think every moment of every day. Thoughts are presented to us constantly from a multitude of sources. We choose which ones we will actually think. We can reject any thought that comes to our mind, or we can hold onto it. We get to choose. Our choices will be reflected in the life we live. Choosing well results in the life God intended you to have, full of power and positive influence in the world. Finally brethren, what you think really matters to God and to your fellow man. Think right thoughts. It's going to bring life to your soul.

"Positive minds--minds full of faith and hope--produce positive lives. Negative minds--minds full of fear and doubt-- produce negative lives." Joyce Meyer

Tip for the day: Take responsibility for your thoughts today like never before. Make every thought positive, life-giving, and God-pleasing. This is the "finally" in Paul's letter to the Philippians. It's my "finally" for you. God bless you as you continue to fill up with His Word, and you will know, as I do, that God loves you and wants what is best for you. I pray that you will experience life at its fullest and overflow with life to everyone you meet.

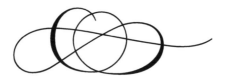

A to Z: Verses and Suggested Declarations

A. *Ask, and ye shall receive, that your joy may be full. John 16:24 (KJV)*
We pray, we ask God our questions, and we receive joy. God answers my prayers and my questions and gives me joy.

B. *Blessed be the Lord, Who daily loads us with benefits, even the God of our salvation! Psalm 68:19 (NKJV)*
I am continually more aware of God's blessings in my life.

C. *Cast all your care upon Him, for He cares for you. I Peter 5:7 (paraphrase)*
I cast my cares on Jesus, giving Him all of my worries, concerns, and fears.

D. *Delight in the Lord, and he will give you the desires of your heart. Psalm 37:4 (NIV)*
I delight in the Lord, and He gives me the desires of my heart.

E. *Enter into his gates with thanksgiving, and into his courts with praise: be thankful unto him, and bless his name. Psalm 100:4 (KJV)*
My praise and thanksgiving take me into the Presence of God. I praise God continually.

F. *For God so loved the world, that he gave his only begotten Son, that whosoever believeth in him should not perish, but have everlasting life. John 3:16 (KJV)*
I believe Jesus is the Son of God, and I have eternal life beginning right now.

G. *God has not given us a spirit of fear, but of power and of love and of a sound mind. 2 Timothy 1:7 (NKJV)*
God gives me a spirit of power, love, and a sound mind.

H. *He sent his word, and healed them, and delivered them from their destructions. Psalm 107:20 (KJV)*
God's Word in me heals me, delivers me, and sets me free.

I. *If ye are willing and obedient, ye shall eat the good of the land. Isaiah 1:19 (NKJV)*
I am willing and obedient, and I am in position to receive God's best for me.

J. *Jesus called the Twelve together and gave them power and authority over all the demons and to heal diseases. Luke 1:9 (ISV)*
God has given me power and authority to do His Will on the earth. In His name, I cast out demons and heal sicknesses according to His perfect will.

K. *Keep your heart with all diligence for that is where your life comes from. Proverbs 4:23 (paraphrase)*
I keep God's Word in my heart, and His life flows freely through me. I protect my thoughts from anything that does not line up with God's Word.

L. *Let your light so shine before men, that they may see your good works and glorify your father which is in heaven. Matthew 5:16 (KJV)*
With the power of God in me, we pray for others, and they are healed, delivered, and set free, giving glory to God.

M. *A merry heart doeth good like a medicine: but a broken spirit drieth the bones. Proverbs 17:22 (KJV)*
I am happy, not because everything is great and everything is going my way, but because He is great, and He is showing me the way.

N. *Nothing can separate us from God's love. Romans 8:38 (NLT)*
I live in His love every day because nothing can separate me from God's love.

O. *Oh, give thanks unto the Lord, for He is good! For His mercy endures forever. Psalm 136:1 (NKJV)*
I continually give thanks to the Lord.

P. *Praise ye the Lord. O give thanks unto the Lord; for he is good: for his mercy endureth for ever. Psalm 106:1 (KJV)*
All day, every day, I live a life of praise.

Q. *Quench not the spirit. Thessalonians 5:19 (KJV)*
The Spirit of God is like a river flowing; I allow that river to flow through me freely.

R. *Rejoice in the Lord always: and again I say, Rejoice. Philippians 4:4 (KJV)*
I choose to rejoice!

S. *O sing unto the Lord a new song: sing unto the Lord, all the earth. Psalm 96:1 (KJV)*
I sing out of my spirit to the Lord, creating a new song.

T. *Trust in the Lord with all thine heart; and lean not unto thine own understanding. In all thy ways acknowledge him, and he shall direct thy paths. Proverbs 3:5,6 (KJV)*
I trust you God, I trust you.

U. *Unto you, O God, do we give thanks. Psalm 75:1 (KJV)*
I continually give thanks to the Lord for He is good.

V. *Verily I say unto you, That whosoever shall say unto this mountain, Be thou removed, and be thou cast into the sea; and shall not doubt in his heart, but shall believe that those things which he saith shall come to pass; he shall have whatsoever he saith. Mark 11:23 (KJV)*
I believe that what I say in line with God's Will comes to pass in my life.

W. *Whatsoever things ye desire, when ye pray, believe that ye receive them, and ye shall have them. Mark 11:24 (KJV)*
I pray. I believe. I have.

X. *Exalt the Lord our God, and worship at his holy mountain for the Lord our God is holy. Psalm 99:9 (NIV)*
I exalt the Lord for all that He has done for me.

Y. *You are the light of the world. A city that is set on a hill cannot be hidden. Matthew 5:14 (NKJV)*
I let the love of God shine through me.

Z. *Not by might nor by power, but by My Spirit. Zechariah 4:6 (KJV)*
I rely on the spirit of God to accomplish all that He wants to accomplish in my life.

Power Verse 1

I can do all things through Christ who strengthens me. Philippians 4:13 (KJV)

I can do all things through Christ who strengthens me.

Power Verse 2

If you abide in Me, and My words abide in you, you shall ask what you will, and it shall be done unto you. John 15:7 (KJV)

I abide in Him, and I receive the answers I need.

Power Verse 3

Thou wilt keep him in perfect peace, whose mind is stayed on thee: because he trusteth in thee. Isaiah 26:3 (KJV)

I focus on Jesus, and He gives me peace.

Power Verse 4

There are six things the LORD hates—no, seven things he detests:

haughty eyes, a lying tongue, hands that kill the innocent, a heart that plots evil, feet that race to do wrong, a false witness who pours out lies, a person who sows discord in a family. Proverbs 6:16-19 (NLT)

I know what God hates, and I turn my back on those things.

Power Verse 5

Finally, brethren, whatsoever things are true, whatsoever things are honest, whatsoever things are just, whatsoever things are pure, whatsoever things are lovely, whatsoever things are of good report; if there be any virtue, and if there be any praise, think on these things. Philippians 4:8 (KJV)

I always choose right thoughts.

And that's it. Any day that we choose any one of these verses and renew our mind to its truth will be a day lived by His spirit. Each day we yield to the spirit a little more is a better day than the one before it. Let's go for it!

Keep our friends close to your heart, and they will keep you close to the heart of God! Then you can enjoy your own Amazing Adventure!

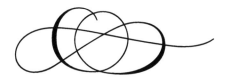

Extreme Adventure

And now for the Extreme Adventure if you're up for it...

Step 1: Decide what day of the week you will start.

Step 2: On that day, begin with A, read the devotional. Instead of picking up a new verse the next day, spend seven days with that same verse. That's the verse of the week, and you simply meditate it as much as you can, still trying to do 100 a day.

Step 3: Write or print the verse of the week on a card, and keep it where you can see it often throughout the day. The more time you spend with the verse, the more energized you will be. Go Extreme for Jesus, and be a blessing everywhere you go. The world needs you!

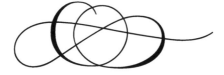

αℱℂα Students

(Dates are year ending)

- Alex Green (2004-2006)
- Ali Mahaffey (2003-2006)
- Amanda Lancaser (2004-2006)
- Amanda McAttee (2002-2003)
- Andrew Miller (2004-2006)
- Ashley Lockhart (2003-06)
- Austin Rabon (2005-2006)
- Bennett Cooley (2004-2006)
- Blade Chaney (2005-2006)
- Brandon Brown (2005-2006)
- Brittany Taylor (2002)
- Brittany Mahaffey (2003-2006)
- Brittany Byerly (2002)

- Caleb Griffin (2004-2006)
- Chandler Leab (2002-06)
- Charity Tillotson (2002)
- Charli Tedder (2003)
- Dallas Taylor (2003)
- Danielle French (2002-2003)
- Desiray Simmons (2003-06)
- Dustin Ray (2002)
- Eric Hopkins (2003-2006)
- Grace Cooley (2006)
- Grace Mason (2003-2006)
- Guerin Feimster (2005)
- Hailey French (2002-2003)
- Hannah Cooley (2005-2006)
- Hayden Tedder (2002-2003)
- Heather Dorsett 2004-2005)
- Holly Manus (2005)
- Hope Mason (2005-2006)
- Isaac Russell (2006)
- Janessa Graham (2003)
- Jared Allen (2002)
- Jay Jordan (2002-2006)
- Jordan Gallman (2005-2006)
- Jordan Green (2004-2006)
- Josh Dorsett (2002-2006)
- Joy Sutton (2002-2003)
- Justin Taylor (2002)
- Kaitlyn Simmons (2006)

- Katherine Gourley (2002)
- Katherine Thompson (2004-2005}
- Katie Brindley (2003-2006)
- Kendall Pittman (2005)
- Kyle Rodgers (2002-2003)
- Laura Huffaker (2003-2004)
- Leah Brindley (2003-2006)
- Logan Foltz (2006)
- Mary Baker (2002-2003)
- Matthew Graham (2002-2003)
- Matt Russell (2003-2004, 2006)
- Melissa Yandell (2005)
- Mitch Wettle (2003-2005)
- Megan Trexler (2002)
- Molly Trexler (2002)
- Monica Allen (2002)
- Nick Jordan (2002-2006)
- Nicole Hopkins (2003-2006)
- R.J. Gallman (2005-2006)
- Raven Foltz (2006)
- Raymond Thanos (2002)
- Rebecca Brindley (2004-2006)
- Robby Russell (2003)
- Robert Barr (2005-2006)
- Samantha West (2006)
- Shelby Tedder (2002-2003)
- Steven Hawk (2003)
- Sydney West (2003-2006)

Sharon Jordan

- Tara Lancaster (2004-2005)
- Taylor Green (2004-2005)
- Taylor Leab (2002-2005)
- Tori Lancaster (2004-2006)
- Trevor Simmons (2006)
- Tyler Yandell (2005-2006)

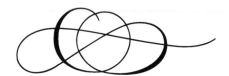

Our Teachers

- Hope Tillotson-Principal (2002)
- Maryjane Mote (2003-2006)
- Angie French (2003-2004)
- Paige Gallman (2005-2006)
- PJ Lancaster (2004-2005)
- Tonia McKinney (2005)
- Rebecca Cooley (2005-2006)
- Shanda West (2006)

Our Part-Time Teachers and Support Team

- Angela Brindley
- Barbara Samayoa
- Cathy Tedder
- Carolyn Dorsett
- Jim Tedder
- Joey Mahaffey
- Kelly Foltz
- Kim Green
- Rick Dorsett
- Robin Whitley
- Ryan Songer
- Steve West
- Tony Green

Thank you!

...for all for the gifts you brought us. Thank you to every parent and grandparent, aunt, uncle, cousin, and friend. You were a part of the vision to raise up Ambassadors for Christ, a royal priesthood, a holy generation. Last, but not least, thank you to the pastors and staff of Agape Faith Church who gave us the support, resources, and opportunity to be an important part of the church vision to strengthen families, better the community and affect the world. God bless you all!

If any names are missing or dates wrong, it was not intentional. Please feel free to contact me at daretobehappytoday@yahoo.com. To connect with others, please look for our Facebook group, "The Amazing A to Z Scripture Adventure." I would love to hear from you.

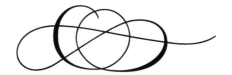

Photos